Beginning With
COCKATIELS

By Anne Ray Streeter

Photographs by Wayne Wallace
(except as indicated otherwise)

Distributed in the UNITED STATES by T.F.H. Publications, Inc., 211 West Sylvania Avenue, Neptune City, NJ 07753; in CANADA by H & L Pet Supplies Inc., 27 Kingston Crescent, Kitchener, Ontario N2B 2T6; Rolf C. Hagen Ltd., 3225 Sartelon Street, Montreal 382 Quebec; in ENGLAND by T.F.H. Publications Limited, 4 Kier Park, Ascot, Berkshire SL5 7DS; in AUSTRALIA AND THE SOUTH PACIFIC by T.F.H. (Australia) Pty. Ltd., Box 149, Brookvale 2100 N.S.W., Australia; in NEW ZEALAND by Ross Haines & Son, Ltd., 18 Monmouth Street, Grey Lynn, Auckland 2 New Zealand; in SINGAPORE AND MALAYSIA by MPH Distributors (S) Pte., Ltd., 601 Sims Drive, # 03/07/21, Singapore 1438; in the PHILIPPINES by Bio-Research, 5 Lippay Street, San Lorenzo Village, Makati Rizal; in SOUTH AFRICA by Multipet Pty. Ltd., 30 Turners Avenue, Durban 4001. Published by T.F.H. Publications Inc. Manufactured in the United States of America by T.F.H. Publications, Inc.

Contents

Overleaf: 1. Before buying a cockatiel, take advantage of the many
books on parrots offered at the pet store, to make sure all your
questions are answered. 2. Cockatiels make affectionate pets, just
as they are affectionate toward one another.

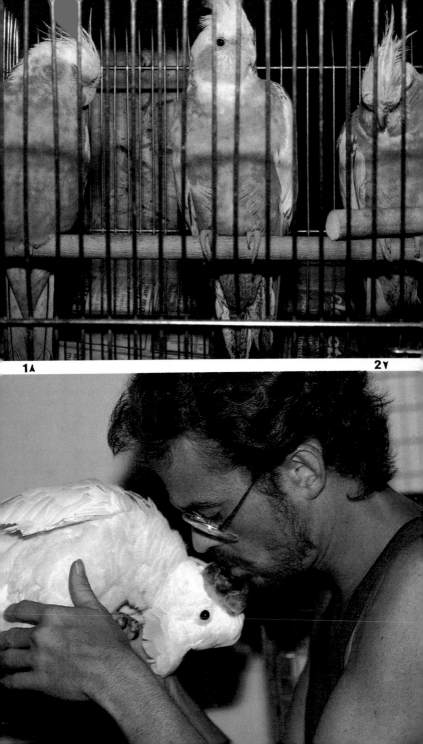

Foreword

When offered the opportunity to write a guide to owning a cockatiel, I gladly accepted. Though I am not a true expert in the subject area, it was felt that as a long-time journalist, I would be more likely to seek answers to the types of questions people would ask about cockatiels.

Besides, I was already hooked on cockatiels as the perfect pet for the fast-paced lifestyle of a working husband and wife living in a relatively confined area.

My first experience with cockatiels came while living in a condominium in Honolulu where the only pets allowed were birds and fish. I had three cockatiels, but I had never picked up a book on or asked a question on how to care for them. I figured instinctively I'd know what to do for them.

That was my mistake — a mistake I hope to prevent you from making.

Though the cockatiels seemed to do well for a time, in spite of my ignorance in caring for them, the full potential of a relationship with these affectionate, charming parrots was missed because I didn't know how to properly win the birds' trust and love. I eventually lost interest and two of the birds escaped from an open window while the third died for unknown reasons.

Overleaf: 1. Pet stores usually have a selection of cockatiels available for sale. 2. Some authorities believe that the cockatiel is the connecting link between the parakeet and the stockier cockatoos, one of which is shown here with John Smithers of Key West's Birds of Paradise pet shop.

This time around, I did my homework. I checked with the experts at the local pet stores and I called respected breeders and veterinarians. I read several of the informative books on cockatiels found at the pet stores and the local library.

Then I applied my new-found knowledge and went bird shopping. I found a lovely pearl-colored female cockatiel — named "Pearl" — who is now a cherished pet in my household. Together, this bird and I learned how to trust one another; how to enjoy each other's company. Given the lifespan of a cockatiel of about 20 years, I hope that by following all that I've learned, Pearl and I will have many years of companionship.

I owe much of what I included in this book to the following persons in Key West, Florida, truly a paradise for parrots: Joe Pigeon and John Smithers, aviculturists and owners of *Birds of Paradise* pet store; Madonna Stedman from *Pampered Pets;* Geraldine Voight of *Bee's Birds;* Herb Martin, an avid breeder of all types of parrots; and Dr. Alan Bush, a veterinarian who specializes in birds. Without their patience, and their knowledge, Pearl and I could never have become friends, and this book would not provide you with what I hope is helpful information in cultivating a friendship with the cockatiel you select.

Overleaf: Delicate coloring makes the lutino one of the most popular cockatiel varieties.

1 ▶
2 ▶

3 ▶
4 ▶

Why a Cockatiel?

The graceful cockatiel with its snappy gold and gray crest and its pert, bright personality makes the ideal pet for those who would like an affectionate bird capable of mimicking words and whistles — a bird who doesn't require much space and is easy to care for.

Read any book about parrots and you'll find it repeatedly said that the cockatiel ranks right up there with the parakeet (budgerigar) as the most popular bird to own. And it's no wonder. These medium-sized Australian parrots are easily tamed and trained if obtained at a young age (less than a year old — the younger the better).

For those who would like to breed birds, whether as a hobby or for the profit, the cockatiel is a prolific bird when matched with the right mate and in the right environment.

The price is right as well. Rather than spend hundreds of dollars for a larger member of the parrot family, the cockatiel can be purchased at a price ranging from about $50 to $100, depending on the color and age of the bird, what area of the country you live in and where you buy the bird.

Longtime Favorite Pet

The cockatiel has long been a favorite pet, dating back to the explorers who discovered new tropical countries where natives tamed the colorful parrots, treasur-

Overleaf: The cockatiel is just one of the many species of parrots, more of less closely related to (1) the salmon-crested cockatoo, (2) the sulphur-crested cockatoo, (3) the red-and-green macaw, and (4) the black parrot.

ing the birds not only for their companionship but for their plumage as well.

But until the introduction of the Australian budgerigar (parakeet) and cockatiels to Europe in the mid-19th century who bred easily in captivity, parrots were only available for those who could afford to pay big money for them. Since prolific breeding meant the "cockies" and "budgies" as they're called in Europe no longer had to be imported, they were readily available and relatively less expensive than larger, more exotic parrots.

For a long while, neither bird could oust the canary as the most popular bird pet but in the 1930's the budgerigar's reputation for mimicking words and phrases began to spread. Today the number of budgies as cage and aviary birds far outnumbers canaries, with the cockatiel coming in a close second as the most popular pet bird.

Advantages of a Cockatiel

Bird lovers are now beginning to appreciate the advantages of having a cockatiel versus the smaller, less costly budgerigar. The cockatiel's larger size makes for a totally different personality (much like the difference in personalities of a small and large breed of dog). It is a hardier bird with a longer life-span. Budgerigars are said to have an average cage life of about four years whereas many cockatiels live to be 20 with aviary cockatiels living as long as 25 years.

Part of the hardiness of the cockatiel is due to the priorities set by breeders who have been more concerned about consistently producing as many young birds as possible in the shortest amount of time than about developing new color varieties. Now it's not uncommon

Overleaf: No other group of birds today enjoys the popularity of parrots as pets: (1) blue-fronted Amazons; (2) the princess parrot.

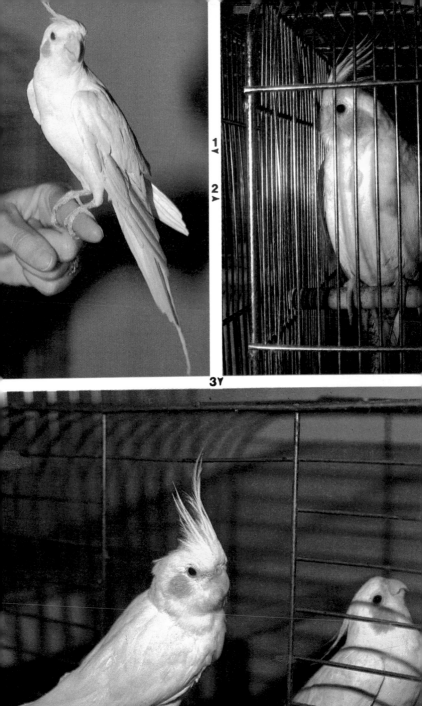

1 ◄
2 ▶

3▼

to hear of cockatiel pairs raising more than a dozen youngsters annually.

If obtained at a young age — the younger the better — cockatiels are easily tamed. They will sit on your finger or shoulder and some love to be caressed just behind the crest.

Easily Trained

They can be trained to mimic melodic whistles and short phrases. One bird who knows how to "talk" can teach another the phrases, but if two cockatiels are placed together — neither of which have been tamed or trained — odds are they'll only be interested in each other and will ignore their owner's attempts at creating a lovable pet.

These colorful parrots will pick up phrases and whistles from sources other than their owner. For example, one apartment-dwelling bird taught another bird in a nearby building its wide range of whistles and phrases — they never saw each other. Another cockatiel who was temporarily being cared for by a woman with many dogs returned home and surprised its owners by mimicking the dog lover's whistle and call for her pets.

One pet store owner used her cockatiel as an advertising gimmick by placing it near the phone. Everytime someone called the store, she would answer with the store's name. Before long, the bird knew the store's name and repeated it often to a respectful crowd of customers.

Easy to Care For

For those who would rather spend their limited leisure time enjoying the benefits of a loving pet rather than always cleaning up after it, the cockatiel is perfect. With the proper cage — one that provides enough room for

Overleaf: The lutino cockatiel (1, 3) was first bred in Florida in 1958 by Cliff Barringer. The pearl (2) is another popular variety.

the bird to spread its wings and plenty of perches and grillwork for climbing on — the cockatiel is at home. One needs daily to change the bird's water and seed, and place new paper in the bottom of the cage — a process which takes less than five minutes to complete.

If you're planning a short trip, the bird is easily cared for by neighbors who can either take the bird to their home for attention or pay a daily visit to the bird. Though there are five-day water dishes available at pet stores, along with covered self-feeders for seed to enable a bird owner to stay away for at least a few days, it is generally recommended that these items not be used.

Water and food can be dirtied by the bird's defecations and various harmful bacteria can grow in the water and in soft foods. A messy cage bottom can also lead to disease. And, as one pet store owner noted, a lonely bird is like a child — it is more likely to get into trouble by knocking over its dishes or injuring itself in some way. A few days without food or water or an injury with bleeding can quickly kill a neglected cockatiel.

What a cockatiel needs most of all is attention. This is particularly true of the single bird in a cage who has been tamed and thus thrives on the affection it receives from its owner. One pet store owner recommends to all new bird owners that they keep a radio playing softly (not hard rock!) when no one is at home just to keep a single cockatiel company. Playing peaceful classical music may help calm down the new bird or one who has had a stressful upset, perhaps weakening its resistance to various health problems. (Several bird owners recommended playing classical music since their birds seemed to be soothed by the works of Bach, Beethoven and Mozart.)

Overleaf: Recently developed mutations include the pearl cockatiel, with its flecks of yellow.

Social Benefits

Cockatiel owners stick together "like birds of a feather." Just walk out of a pet store with your new cockatiel or mention to someone you've joined the growing number of cockatiel owners and you'll be amazed at how others will offer stories about their own "baby."

One woman visiting Key West from Arkansas raved about her four-year-old pet to a new owner who had just come from the pet shop, cage in hand. She offered all kinds of helpful information on what worked for her bird. One of the best compliments she paid her bird was that it made a terrific watchdog for a single woman, alerting her of any possible intruder with its unique high-pitched "kreech" whistle.

In some areas of the country there are bird clubs comprised of novice and expert alike. Such clubs may have bird shows, enabling you to not only meet other enthusiasts but to observe the varieties of cockatiels available. Joining such a club is a good way to meet others with common interests, and to gather the latest information on whatever questions you may have about your new pet. Check with a pet store, veterinarian or breeder to see if there's a club in your area. If there isn't, you might consider starting one for yourself.

Variety of Ways to Care for Your Bird

One thing you're certain to find, whether you use the advice provided by a pet store, breeder or veterinarian, each bird owner will have his or her own methods of taming and training a bird, clipping its wings or nails,

Overleaf: 1. A pair of normal-colored cockatiels. 2. Make sure the environment chosen for your new cockatiel doesn't include unscreened doors and windows or drafty areas. 3. If you have young children or pets that might hurt the bird, consider hanging the cage out of reach. 4. A single caged bird will depend on you for companionship.

feeding the bird or caring for it when it's ill or injured. Each of the methods must have worked for them or they wouldn't be doing it.

Perhaps the key to success is recognizing that your bird is unique. Each bird is an individual and responds to various treatments in different ways. He may enjoy an apple or orange without any coaxing or he may be satisfied with a well-balanced variety of seeds and grain supplemented with table food. Taming may come as quickly as the first 15 minutes of your relationship or it may require a few days of patient coaxing. If you choose to breed your bird, it may adapt readily to the selected mate, or, as with humans, the mate may be totally unsuitable for your bird.

Respect your bird. Learn its habits and, though it will usually adapt to your lifestyle, make sure you stay tuned in to its routine. If your bird's usual routine differs — a change in eating or singing patterns, apathy, puffed up feathers or runny eyes and nose for example — check its environment to see if it's reacting to something new and stressful that can be quickly remedied or consider taking it to a veterinarian to see what's wrong.

With just a minimum of caring concern and love on your part, the cockatiel provides its owners with years of friendship filled with their playful antics and affectionate manners. That's why the cockatiel is more frequently recommended for first-time bird owners.

Overleaf: Cockatiels require a lot of attention and will enjoy toys like this Nylabird dumbbell.

What Is a Cockatiel?

The Australian cockatiel is the lone sample of its genus, *Nymphicus hollandicus,* and is said by some to be the connecting link between the stockier, larger cockatoo and its smaller counterpart, the parakeet.

The first scientific description came from the scientist Gmelin in his work *Systema naturae* who called the bird a "wedge-tailed cockatoo" or "cockatoo parakeet" (*Psittacus novae-hollandiae*); since then the scientific name has been changed.

The cockatiel is a member of the parrot or "psittacine" order, possessing the characteristic hooked beak, short neck and curious feet — two toes pointing forward and two pointing backward. Other members of the order include budgerigars, macaws, Amazon parrots, lovebirds and lories.

Some authorities believe the cockatiel is the smallest member of the cockatoo family. The cockatiel shares the distinctive erectile crest of its larger counterparts and the limited colorations. You'll never see a cockatoo or cockatiel with blue, green or purple feathers as with other parrots.

Overleaf: 1. Before buying a bird, ask yourself if you're ready for a commitment which includes both time and money to ensure that your bird is housed in a proper cage, fed a proper diet, and cared for by a veterinarian, should the need arise. 2. A reputable pet store is perhaps the best place to begin your search for a healthy cockatiel. If you will be taking your bird home in its cage, be sure to cover it.

Coloration

Instead, the plumage of the more common cockatiel will be smokey gray in color with a wide band of white along its wings. Mature males display a bright yellow head with orange patches over the ears. The upper side of the tail is pearl gray, the underside black.

Immature males and females have a yellow and black banding on the underside of the tail with facial yellow restricted to outlining the features. The young males begin to show color change at about six months of age with the entire head turning rapidly to yellow.

In recent years, breeders have developed a variety of color mutations, introducing lighter variations of yellow, cinnamon and gray.

Cockatoo vs Cockatiel

There are major differences in the cockatoo and cockatiel. A cockatoo is larger, stockier, possessing a short tail and massive bill. The cockatiel is daintier in size and build, measuring about 12 inches from the top of its head to the tip of its long tail (about half of the bird's total body length is due to its tail).

The cockatoo feeds on seeds and fruit and because of its bill is capable of eating even those foods that have an extremely hard shell. In its natural habitat, the cockatoo can dig for tubers, bulbs and other buried vegetables.

In the Wild

In its natural habitat in Australia, the cockatiel is a nomadic bird that searches for seeds and water in the more arid central areas of that continent. Its small size and determined flight enables it to fly great distances at

Overleaf: If you acquire a second cockatiel, your pet bird will soon turn its interest to its new companion.

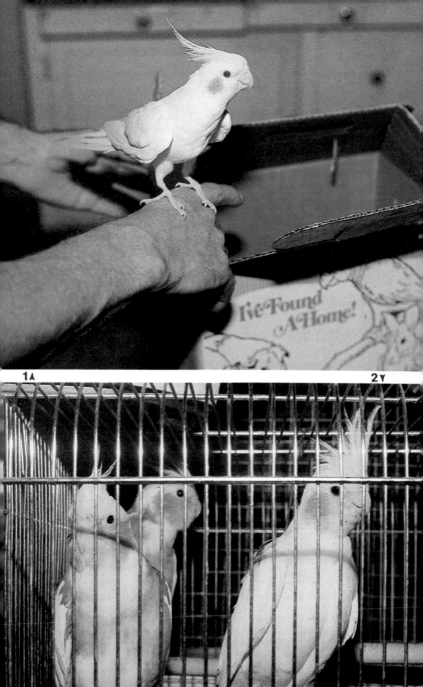

I've Found A Home!

quick speeds in search of food and water. Because it often finds its food on the ground, its coloration blends in with the landscape. The cockatiel is capable of quickly escaping any would-be predator.

The cockatiel was described in detail by the English ornithologist John Gould who went to Australia in the 1840s to compile books on the profusion of colorful parrots found on that continent.

Gould was credited with bringing the first live budgerigars out of Australia in 1840 and though no one is certain, it's assumed the importation of cockatiels to Europe began about the same time. The first recorded breedings were in Europe in 1845, according to George Smith, author of *Encyclopedia of Cockatiels*.

The name *cockatiel* was coined later by a Mr. Jamrach, a flourishing importer of exotic livestock into Britain at that time. His choice of name is said to have originated from the Dutch "kakatielje" which was said to have come from the Portuguese for "little cockatoo," or "cacatilho."

Domestication and Breeding

By 1884, the cockatiel was a well-respected breeding bird in European aviaries. In 1902, David Seth-Smith wrote that, with the exception of the budgerigar, the cockatiel was the most common Australian parrot in English aviaries where multitudes were being raised annually. He said his own pair once reared 16 young between March and September.

The domestication of cockatiels in America is lacking in documentation, but it's believed the history of the

Overleaf: 1. Cockatiels may also be transported in cardboard cartons. 2. Make sure that the bird you buy looks healthy and alert. Apathy may mean the bird is too sick to care about what's going on around it.

bird in North America is similar to that of Europe with one major exception — the cockatiel seems to have received a greater reception as a cage bird in America and South Africa than in Europe where the greater majority were favored for aviaries, particularly once color mutations began to evolve, making the bird a more desirable one for aviculturists.

Following World War II, there was a considerable amount of inbreeding of the cockatiel in Europe, Africa and America. This inbreeding soon resulted in radically different color mutations.

According to Smith, one of the first color mutations which began appearing in the 1950s was a "pied" bird, sometimes also referred to as a "harlequin" for its spots of light and dark colors. Unfortunately, documentation on avian mutations is lacking so no records exist of this variation's early history.

In 1958 the first "lutino" cockatiels with their yellow-colored feathers were bred in captivity by Cliff Barringer in Florida.

With the development of these and other variations that have persevered, breeding became big money. By the 1960s, knowledgeable breeders began acquiring any abnormally colored bird they could find. The Dutch and Belgians are largely responsible for developing the deep canary shade of the selected lutinos and they aided in the development of the "pearled" or "laced" variety which originated in West Germany in 1967.

Overleaf: 1. If you are planning to train a bird, the younger it is when you purchase it, the better. If you wait until a bird has acquired the bright yellow head and cheeks shown here, to ensure that you have a male, you will lose valuable training time. 2. Leg bands are one of the principal means used to identify birds. 3. When transporting a bird, be careful not to leave it in a car that is too hot or too cold. Keep it covered to protect it from drafts and other disturbances.

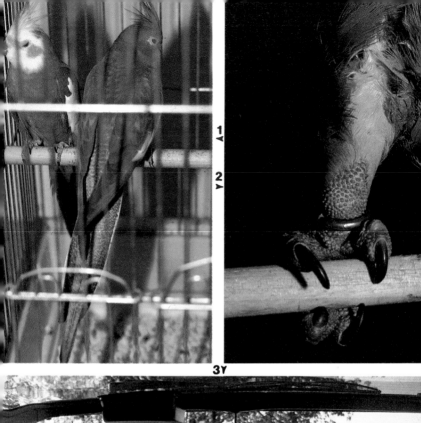

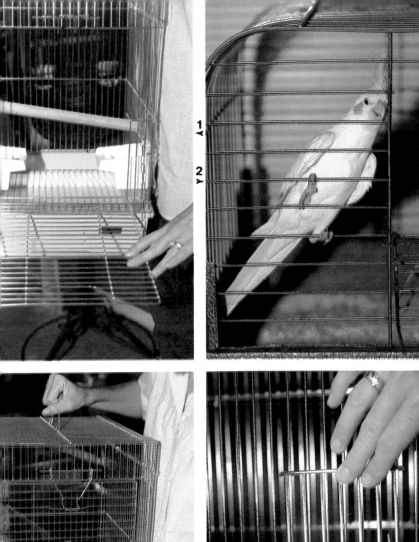

The cinnamon was discovered the following year, in 1968, in Belgium and the red-eyed or fallow the year after, 1969.

The efficiency of the breeders who used increased knowledge of genetics to produce great quantities of the European-produced variations quickly caused the high-priced market for the cockatiel to collapse by 1975. No more did these birds fetch astronomically high rates, though the price of any color forms purchased directly from a European breeder is about two to three times more than the cost of the more common gray cockatiel. The fallow or red-eyed silver variety fetches a price 10 times more than the value of a normal bird.

The heavy emphasis these past few years on breeding mutations has benefited the cockatiel and fellow parrots by turning a hit-and-miss process into a science. Great consideration was given to the proper nutrition of the parrot and its chicks and to the appropriate nesting facilities. The attention given these birds resulted in even hardier varieties capable of producing greater numbers of young that survive to become, hopefully, someone's cherished pet.

Overleaf: 1. If possible, have your bird's cage ready before placing the bird inside. The cage should have a door big enought to bring the bird out on your hand easily. 2. Horizontal wiring makes it easy for the cockatiel to climb around. Make sure the cage is roomy enough that the bird can stretch its wings without touching the sides. 3. A grid over the papered cage tray keeps the bird from walking in its droppings and makes it easier to change the paper daily. 4. Food and water cups should be readily accessible for daily attention.

The Cockatiel as a Pet

If all that's been said thus far about the cockatiel as the perfect pet appeals to you, ask yourself the following questions before racing out to buy one:

1) Do you or other family members have the time to spend in cultivating the friendship of this bird? A single caged cockatiel will depend on you for its companionship. It is a sociable bird, and if you don't have the time to talk and play with it, then perhaps you should consider buying another type of bird or a pair of cockatiels who will keep each other company.

2) Is the environment where the bird will be placed an appropriate one? If there are a lot of windows or drafts, special precautions will need to be taken to prevent your bird from being chilled. If you have other pets, particularly a cat, then the bird's cage will need to be placed out of reach, preferably hanging from the ceiling. Caution must be taken to keep doors and windows closed or screened to keep the bird from escaping. And young children must be instructed on how to treat the bird. A cockatiel, though an affectionate bird once tamed, can be easily injured by a groping youngster. Out of fear, an adult cockatiel will likely bite the child, an unnecessary situation which can be avoided if the proper care is taken.

Overleaf: 1. A brood of recently hatched cockatiels (photo by John Daniel). 2. A young lutino cockatiel—on youngsters the crest is often not very full (photo by Dr. Herbert R. Axelrod).

1▲　　　　　　2▼

3) Are you committed to being attentive to the bird's needs? Though the feeding and cleaning of a bird's cage takes hardly any time at all, it is of critical importance to the bird's health that this routine be conducted daily. Just as humans must eat and drink uncontaminated food from clean dishes to protect themselves from illness, so do birds. Harmful bacteria and molds can grow in damp food left too long in a bird's dish. The bird's droppings can contaminate the food and water supply and, if the cage bottom is not covered with clean paper each day, the dried droppings can blow around, courting potential health hazards.

If the bird will be left alone for longer than a day or two, it is advisable to have someone check on the bird daily or else you could take the bird in its cage to someone's home where the proper attention can be provided.

The commitment to pay attention to the bird means learning the cockie's habits so that when its routine suddenly changes, you'll be tuned in enough to know there's a problem that must be remedied in a hurry. A sick bird will fake normalcy as long as possible, reacting instinctively to the law of the wild where the weakest bird falls prey to its enemies. By the time the symptoms of illness can no longer be hidden by a bird, it's often too late for even the best of veterinarians to return the bird to good health.

4) After the initial investment of between $50 and $100 to buy the bird, are you prepared to spend what it takes to provide the cockatiel with an adequate cage, a well-balanced diet and medical attention as required? As with any pet, there is a commitment involved to care

Overleaf: 1. Mirrors are not advisable if you plan to teach the bird to talk—the bird will pay attention to its reflection, not you. 2. The cage should have a variety of perches. Branches with natural bark will provide needed nutrients.

for it. It can't be just turned loose and expected to live a healthy life. Some of the costs involved include the price of a cage that is large enough for a cockatiel to spread its wings in without touching the edges of the cage; a high-quality mixture of seeds and cereal grains as well as nutritional supplements that provide the necessary vitamins and minerals; possible veterinarian fees, particularly if you follow their recommendation of taking a newly-purchased bird to the vet for a physical exam followed by annual check-ups to assure the bird is in good health.

5) What do you want the bird for? This is an important question for the answer could determine whether you buy one or more birds, male or female. For example, if the cockie is to be a pet in the truest sense of the word, it is best to buy one bird so it will learn to focus its attention on you and other family members. A single caged bird may be trained to talk or whistle and will gladly sit on your finger or shoulder while you carry out your business.

Add another bird, and, no matter how tame that first bird was, it is likely to turn its attention to its feathered friend, teaching it all that it knows or sometimes, just forgetting all those phrases and whistles learned after many patient hours of training.

If the bird is to be alone most of the time and is wanted more for its beauty in a cage or aviary, perhaps buying a second cockatiel or even other types of birds such as parakeets or finches would be wise.

If breeding is the purpose for purchasing a cockatiel, then, of course, an additional bird or birds must be ob-

Overleaf: A variety of foods are needed by cockatiels to meet their nutritional needs. Start with a good seed mix, available at your pet store.

tained along with the other necessary items for successful breeding and nesting.

After considering these questions, if it is determined
that a cockatiel is still the pet desired, then begins the
search for the perfect companion.

Buying a Cockatiel

There are many ways of locating and buying a cockatiel. Perhaps the most common place to start is the local
pet store where you're likely to find someone qualified
to answer any of the questions typically raised by a nervous new owner. Buying from a pet store assures that
when you leave with your bird, you'll be well-equipped
with the proper cage and other necessities. And a reputable pet store will be there to answer questions about the
bird once you get it home, particularly if for some
reason, the bird becomes ill in the first few days.

Another good source is a breeder who knows exactly
when the bird was born and can attest to its upbringing,
thus assuring the bird did not spend its early days in a
crowded quarantine cage with hundreds of other birds,
some of which may have carried a potentially fatal disease.

Veterinarians are good to contact for they will most
likely be able to recommend a good breeder or pet store
reputed to have healthy birds. Ask friends who have
birds, or, if there is a local bird club, attend a meeting to
find out where they recommend purchasing your pet.

Most of these sources are listed in the phone book and
some even run advertisements in the classified sections
of the local newspaper, particularly when there's a
recently hatched clutch that will soon be ready for sale.

Overleaf: 1. Spray millet hung in the cage provides a nutritious
treat. 2. Situating your bird's cage in the kitchen near the stove
must be avoided.

Finding a Healthy Bird

When looking at potential cockatiel candidates, follow these guidelines in determing which bird is the best bet:

1) Does it look healthy?

A healthy bird will be bright and alert. Don't be fooled into thinking that an apathetic bird is tame. It may be so sick that it could not care less about any potential dangers. On the other hand, a candidate for taming may stand out in the crowd of its cage mates by continuing to calmly perform its natural functions such as eating and preening itself even while being watched from outside of the cage.

A bird with ruffled feathers in a sleeping posture that is not easily aroused or one with a runny nose or eyes or an injured appendage is also not a good bet. The plumage should be smooth and, with the exception of perhaps the crown, there should be no bare spots.

Have the salesperson check the breast of the cockatiel to determine if it's plump and round rather than sharp and emaciated, indicating an unhealthy bird. It is also unwise to buy a bird that has moist or caked wet droppings on the underside of its tail or whose droppings are not dark green and white and in good form — all indicators of an intestinal disease.

Respiration should not be labored and irregular but rather slow and even. Missing toes or claws are not a problem, unless the wound is fresh or there's a swelling in the area.

Determining the Age

2) How old is the bird?

It is difficult to tell the exact age of a bird, hence the

Overleaf: Plants such as poinsettia (1) and pets such as cats (2) are potential dangers to pet cockatiels.

1▲

2▼

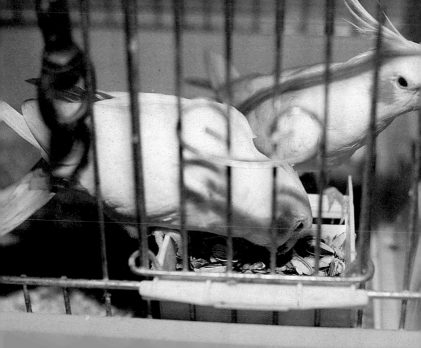

need to be able to trust what the pet store owner, vet or breeder tells you about the birds. But the age plays an important factor in selection if the reason for having the bird is to tame it and make it into a loveable companion.

Optimally, it is best to get a cockatiel at a very young age, preferably between the ages of 10 and 16 weeks of age. Birds that have been completely or partly hand-reared and thus trust the close human relationship are the easiest to befriend.

A cockatiel that already has a bright yellow head is at least six months old, and though it is possible to make a pet from an older bird, it is more time-consuming and difficult. Another guide to determining age on all but the lutino birds is to check the skin surrounding and composing the nostrils. This area, the cere, is pink in fledglings and darkens to gray-black in just a few months. The lutino always sports a flesh-pink cere, regardless of age. Also, the feathers of a normal cockatiel are much darker in the adult, which may also provide a clue to the bird's true age.

Determining Sex

3) Does it matter whether it's a male or female?

Both the male and female cockatiel possess equal potential in being a perfect pet and both will learn to talk. But the male is usually preferred, partly because they are the more colorful and attractive, but also due to the persistent and unfounded myth that females do not talk and are harder to tame.

Overleaf: 1. Veterinarians specializing in birds recommend taking your new bird for a physical exam soon after you've acquired it. Afterwards, annual physicals will help to keep the bird in top health. 2. Parrots are creatures of habit, ignoring anything they're not used to, including food. Offer fresh vegetables and fruits regularly to give your bird a chance to develop a taste for a diverse diet.

If a buyer waits until patches of yellow begin to appear on the young male's head to assure a male is purchased, valuable training time that may never be recovered is lost. You'd be better off buying a young cockie regardless of its sex to assure the bird is tamable and trainable.

If breeding is the game plan, then buying two adults who have their full color array of plumage and fully developed bodies is probably a better idea since it is easier to tell the difference between males and females. In the normal adult grays, one method used in telling the difference is to examine their tail feathers — males have dark gray tail plumage while females have flecks of yellow throughout.

It's not as easy to sex the new color mutations such as the white lutinos and the cinnamon. Finding a pearly adult male for breeding is also difficult since a male pearl loses its yellow flecks of color as it turns a year old, looking more like a normal gray than pearly. The female doesn't lose her speckles of color.

Tagged Birds
4) Is the bird tagged?

There are varying opinions on the importance of buying a bird with an identification tag on its leg. Herb Martin, an avid parrot breeder in Key West, tags each new chick with a seamless band that has an identification number and birth date.

If your bird has an ID bracelet, record its number for safekeeping. This makes it easier to identify your bird should it be caged with others, at the vet's for example, or if it is stolen or lost and found by a stranger.

Overleaf: Cockatiels are sociable—a bird kept singly as a pet will be affectionate towards its owner (1), transferring the affection it would otherwise show toward another cockatiel (2).

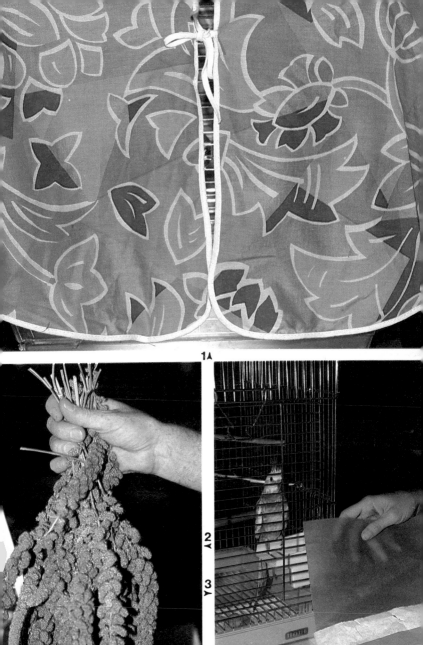

1▶

2▶

3▶

Taking the Bird Home

Getting your bird home and settled into its new environment with a minimum of stress to the pet is of great importance. The bird should be transported in a covered cage or in the specially-made carrying boxes provided by most pet stores. Some stores even place cockatiels in paper bags, but this could prove to be a bad idea if care is not taken to keep the bird from being injured by someone sitting on the bag or placing a heavy object on top of it.

If it's a cold day, take special care to keep the bird warm, possibly postponing the trip if it's raining since the dampness could lead to a cold. If it's a warm day, however, be sure not to leave the bird in the car with the windows rolled up. The temperature outside of the car may be pleasant enough, but sunlight magnified by the vehicle's glass and metal construction could cause the interior to heat up like an oven, quickly killing the bird.

It is important to keep the bird covered on its way to its new home to protect it from wind and the frightening array of strange sights and sounds. The less stress the better for the bird.

If at all possible, have the bird's new home — cage or

Overleaf: 1. A cage cover provides darkness for rest and will keep potentially harmful drafts out. 2. Birds enjoy spray millet so much it is almost as much a toy as a food. 3. The cage floor should be cleaned daily. For easy cleaning, put in several sheets of paper at a time and each day remove the top one.

aviary — ready for its new occupant. Placing a bird into its new home and then putting all of the needed feeding utensils, toys and the like into the cage will only upset the bird unnecessarily.

Choosing the Proper Cage

Selecting the proper cage is extremely important. The pet store should have a wide selection of sizes and shapes and can recommend those cages that are best for the cockatiel. Just make sure the cage's design complies with the following:

— A wide enough structure to allow the bird to stretch its wings without touching the sides of the cage. The ideal size is at least 26'' x 20'' x 20''. There are some cages on the market today that provide the cockatiel with a playground attached to the door so that when the cage door is open, the bird has a variety of perches, ladders and swings to play on. When the door is closed, the playground folds into the inside of the cage. The idea is a good one, but it's not recommended for a bird who will be in its cage for long stretches — the playground takes up half the flight space needed by the cockatiel to spread its wings.

— Appropriate heavy-wire parrot construction, preferably from stainless steel or non-rusting metal. The more decorative cages made from bamboo or colored with toxic paints are not suitable since the cockatiel like other parrots will simply chew on the harmful material, eventually escaping from the wooden cage. If building a cage, just be certain that non-toxic materials are used and that there are no sharp wires left exposed that might possibly injure the bird.

Overleaf: Various accessories are available to make bird keeping easier. Clips are useful to attach spray millet, greens and the like to the cage bars.

1 ►
2 ►

3 ▼

— A horizontal grill-work design that allows the cockatiel to climb the walls of its cage. Many thinner-wired cages that are suitable for canaries and finches have vertical bars which keep cockatiels from exercising their climbing capabilities.

— A bottom grill to help keep the bird from walking in its own waste. Paper is kept under the grill making it easy to change daily without upsetting the bird.

— A door large enough for you to put your hand in the cage and bring the bird out without touching any point. A small door only makes a bird more nervous about leaving the safety of his cage. Make sure the latch on the doors can't be opened by an industrious cockatiel. Safety locks are available at the pet store to assure your bird stays in its cage until you want to bring it out.

Getting the Cage Ready

The cage should be furnished with feed and water dishes that are easily accessible for daily attention. Some cages provide separate doors through which the water and feed dishes can be refilled without having to place your hand into the cage, disturbing the bird in the process. Other cages place the feeding dishes in a sheltered area protected from the bird's droppings.

Birds love toys such as bells and will happily play for hours. Just be sure the toys provided have no loose parts or clangers that could be swallowed by the bird.

Mirrors are not suggested for the bird if you plan to teach it to talk since the bird will pay attention to its reflection rather than to you.

The cage should have plenty of perches of varying

Overleaf: 1. Commercially available vitamin preparations are recommended by some bird enthusiasts. 2. Products to prevent infestations of lice and mites are also available. 3. Ground corn cob is the floor covering recommended by Key West's Birds of Paradise.

widths so that the bird can move about the cage and exercise its legs and feet. Natural barked woods are great, as long as the wood is from a non-poisonous tree (check with your county agricultural extension office or pet store to be sure the plant you have in mind is suitable for a bird). Make sure the natural perch is washed thoroughly to remove any trace of insecticides.

A special toy for your bird is a fairly new product on the market called Nylabird. These chewable playthings give the bird something to gnaw on that will supply it with its nutritional requirement for calcium, keep it entertained and at the same time, prevent its beak from getting too long. Your pet store or veterinarian can tell you more about Nylabird.

Where to Place the Cage

Before bringing the bird home, decide where to place the cage. Take heed of the following no-no's:

— Keep it away from drafts and windows to keep the bird from getting chilled.

— Don't place it in direct sunlight. It's all right to have some sun in the cage as long as the bird has a shaded area to go to as well.

— In areas where there are changes in the seasons, make sure your bird is placed in a temperature controlled area year around. Don't, however, place it near an open-flamed heater or right in front of a frigid air conditioner.

— Don't place it near poisonous plants such as oleanders, poinsettias or philodendrons where it might nibble on a leaf or two.

— Don't place it near the stove or any place that could prove dangerous if the bird is out of its cage.

Overleaf: Change the bird's water daily; the seed dish should be cleaned at least twice a week.

1▲   2▼

BIRD
BATH

ALL PURPOSE
CAGE CU

BIRD
CAGE CU

PLANIT

— Keep it out of reach of other household pets, particularly cats. Since cats are such ingenious animals when faced with the temptation of a feathered treat, it is best to hang the cage from the ceiling (away from ceiling fans), assuring that there are no nearby areas for the cat to climb to reach the bird. If placed on a shelf, make sure the cat can't knock the cage down, which could result in an open cage door with a waiting cat ready to pounce on the disoriented bird. (My cat had the bird cage on the floor with a very confused bird inside within two hours of bringing the bird home from the store. I thought I had placed the cage in a "safe" place on a bookcase shelf, but obviously I underestimated her determination.)

— Place it out of reach of any young children who might unwittingly let the bird out when no one is around to protect it.

— Don't put a single caged bird in a secluded area, away from human contact. These birds are sociable by nature and deserve to be placed where they'll receive attention from family members.

A word of caution to personal computer users — don't place the cage where the bird is likely to drop seed hulls or spray water right onto your valuable equipment. An accidentally dropped water dish or seed tray could ruin a floppy disc or, even worse, cause irreparable damage to the computer keyboard or terminal or printer. (Because I wanted my bird close by while I worked, I have not followed my own advice, but I do keep my computer covered and the bird's water dish out of range.)

Overleaf: 1. To keep perches clean, use sandpaper or a paint scraper like the one shown here. 2. Accessory baths and cups are available for cages of every size and design.

About Aviaries

It's been said that a cage can never be big enough for a cockie. If you have the room and are planning to have additional birds for their variety or for breeding purposes, then you'll need an aviary.

An indoor aviary can be set up just about anywhere as long as the same guidelines for placement of a cage are followed. Aviaries are easily made from wire mesh and wooden boards. The floor of the room may serve as the cage bottom with a low-placed door included for ease in cleaning. Food dishes should be placed on a shelf halfway up the wall within easy reach of all the birds.

Outdoor aviaries should have a sheltered area and should be constructed to provide for changes in weather, depending on what area you live in. A concrete foundation underneath the structure will prevent rats, mice and snakes from getting in.

The outside flight area can be made from wooden framing and fine wire mesh — as small as possible to keep other unwelcome guests from squeezing in. The sheltered area may be made from bricks, wood or manufactured sheetings. This area should be easily accessible to the birds and should be bright and well-insulated.

Cover the floor of the aviary with gravel. By raking seeds and food remains into the ground periodically, they will germinate, providing the birds with a vitamin-rich dietary supplement. Include a few branches among the perches for the birds to chew on, replacing as necessary. Plant low bushes and shrubs alongside the outer area of the aviary, providing the birds with a feeling of being outdoors.

Overleaf: Bringing a bird to the stage where it is hand-tame is the first step toward training the bird to mimic speech and whistles and to do tricks.

1 ►
2 ►

3 ►

Though placing a bird in an aviary just about guarantees it will never be tameable, many people prefer having birds in their more natural state to enjoy.

Free-Flying Birds

Some cockatiel owners have successfully trained their birds to fly in and out of the home at will, returning to their source of food and for human attention. Such training is risky since the bird is susceptible to such animals as dogs, cats and large birds such as hawks.

Others allow their birds to fly inside the house. Again, this may prove risky since a cockatiel by nature is as inquisitive as a two-year-old child. It will get into dangerous situations and may eat poisonous or harmful substances if you don't keep a constant eye on its whereabouts.

A cockatiel should be allowed out of its cage at least once daily to give it some exercise and to have a chance to interact with you. Returning the bird to the top of the cage or to a special bird playground of ladders and swings nearby will enable it to remain outside of confinement yet safely out of harm's way.

Overleaf: 1. Some cockatiels will accept the kind of bath that can be hooked into the cage-door opening, while others prefer a shower from a plant mister. 2, 3. Bathing is followed by preening, which is the bird's way of keeping its plumage in good condition.

Caring for the Bird

Too often, novice bird fanciers buy their first bird from an unreliable source ill-qualified to provide accurate information on caring for their bird. They leave with a sack of cheap bird seed in hand, thinking that's all their new friend will need for nourishment.

"That's like giving a child a storeful of bakery goods like donuts and cakes — that kind of a diet would only lead to malnourishment and most likely death," warns Florida Keys veterinarian Alan Bush, who is also a bird fancier.

To make sure the bird is healthy and that you understand the importance of caring properly for the bird, Bush recommends making an appointment with a veterinarian who has some experience with birds. Wait a few days after bringing the bird home to give it a chance to get used to its new environment, however.

Most vets will give the bird a physical examination, and will check its droppings to see if they're as firm and properly colored (a bull's-eye shape with dark green center and white outside) as they should be. Some, like Dr. Bush, have literature and short film strips available to provide you with concise, easy to understand techniques on all aspects of caring for your bird.

It's good to establish a relationship with a vet in the

Overleaf: Pearl, after having had her wings clipped, sits on the hand of her new owner, Anne Streeter.

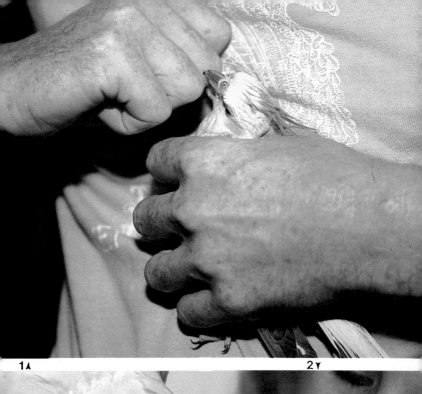

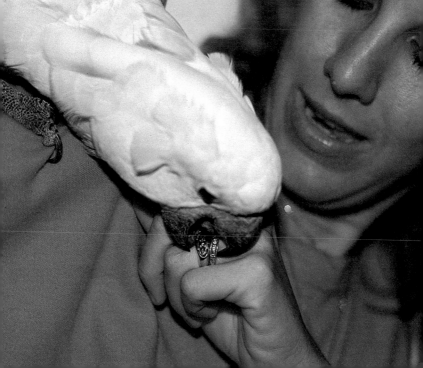

early stages so that if your bird does become sick, you'll have a ready source of assistance. It's also advised that the bird be taken for annual checkups. Such visits could cost from $15 to $20, but once an investment in a pet has been made, its value comes from being alive and healthy.

Nutritional Requirements

Cockatiels should be offered a variety of foods in their diet though their primary nourishment is seeds of various sorts. Remember, their native habitat is the arid central areas of Australia where they foraged for whatever seed, fruit and other foods and water they could find. Their efficient digestion system enables them to utilize every bit of nutrient available from the seeds they eat.

But seed alone does not provide the total vitamin and mineral requirements of these birds, lacking protein with little of the required amino acid lysine as well as vitamins A, D, B-two (riboflavin) and B-twelve (cyanocobalamin) and minerals such as calcium. Since birds in captivity are totally dependent on you to assure they eat properly, it's important that you provide them with a healthy diet.

That may be easier said than done since cockatiels are creatures of habit. If they have been raised with one type of seed alone, the introduction of other foods may cause them to feel threatened. It's like coaxing a young child to eat vegetables — patience and ingenuity are required.

Cockatiel Seed

Commercially-prepared seed mixes for cockatiels are available at most pet stores and it is recommended that seed be purchased in see-through bags so you'll know

Overleaf: Bites from a bird as small as a cockatiel (1) may be painful but are not dangerous. A cockatoo (2), however, has a much more powerful beak—this one is showing a characteristic interest in bright, shiny objects.

what you're getting. These mixes generally are comprised of sunflower seeds, hemp, oats, wheat, peanuts and millet. Every bird has its favorite seeds and will usually scatter those seeds that are distasteful to it.

Hemp should be kept at a minimum since the high oil content could lead to an overweight bird. But it is particularly needed before and during the breeding season and in the colder winter months. The cereal grains, such as oats (hulled and unhulled) and wheat should be included in the diet, but if the bird should gain too much weight, cut back on the amount provided.

A special treat that should be made available at all times is millet sprays, and there are some commercially-produced seed treats such as honeysticks that most cockatiels enjoy.

Fruits, Vegetables

In addition, many cockatiels will develop a liking for fruits and vegetables. Try giving your bird small pieces of apples, pears, carrots, and various berries such as rosehips, rowan and hawthorn. Valuable sources of vitamins are chickweed, dandelion (especially its blossom), carrot leaves, common groundsel, lettuce (romain rather than iceberg) and spinach.

When greenfood is scarce during the winter months, or when birds require additional vitamins such as before and during breeding season, the birds should be given sprouted seeds.

Suggested Diet

A recommended diet should include the following:
— One monkey biscuit (available from the pet store)

Overleaf: Taming, training, and talking all depend on fostering your cockatiel's trust.

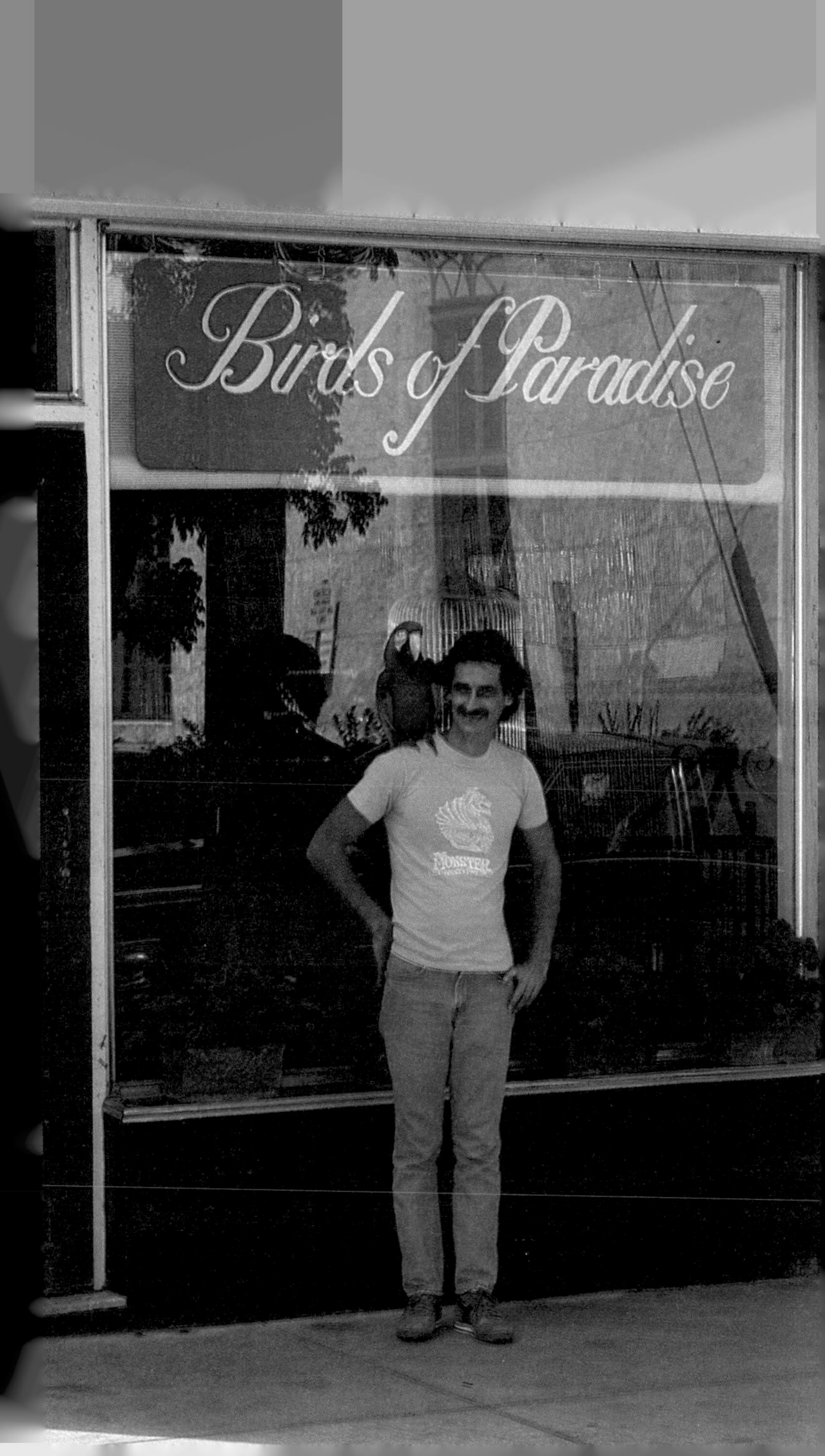
Birds of Paradise

per day, served either dry or soaked for 30 seconds in water or milk (milk provides the needed lysine).

— One tablespoon daily of seed sprouts comprised of 50 percent sunflower seeds and 50 percent small seeds or legumes. The sprouts may be sprinkled with powdered cuttlebone or calcium carbonate. (You can easily sprout your own seeds. Just soak seeds for 24 hours. Drain and rinse them three times and then spread them on a clean towel, leaving them alone for another 24 hours until they just begin to sprout. Before giving the bird these sprouts, rinse them again thoroughly. The sprouts may be stored in the refrigerator for up to a week.)

— One drop of cod liver oil three times a week.

— A small piece of fresh corn cob daily.

— A small pea-size piece of longhorn cheddar cheese daily.

— And, of course, a variety of dried seeds.

Your bird should be fed daily to assure the foods provided have not had time to spoil or be soiled by the bird's droppings. If your cockatiel does not readily accept any food that is new, just keep providing small pieces of it on a regular basis to give him the opportunity to try it. After all, unless the food is made ava   ,, he'll never have the chance to acquire a taste for it.

Natural Bark

Important trace elements and vitamins are available to your bird from chewing on branches and twigs, particularly the bark and the buds of flowers and leaves. A plentiful supply of branches from willow, hazel-nut,

Overleaf: Joe Pigeon, co-owner of Birds of Paradise in Key West, became a bird enthusiast after purchasing a parakeet five years ago. Pretty soon he and his business partner John Smithers had 200 birds in their apartment before opening their pet store. Perched on Joe's shoulder is a macaw named Sinbad.

oak, maple, hibiscus or fruit trees is essential. Just be sure the branches have not been sprayed with insecticide and have been rinsed thoroughly before giving them to your feathered friend.

Necessary calcium can be provided in the form of a Nylabird toy available from a pet store or veterinarian, cuttlebone, calcium and mineral blocks and the grated shells of mussels and eggs are also recommended.

Use of Vitamins

There are varying views of the inclusion of commercially-prepared vitamin preparations. Some trainers advise using vitamins in the bird's drinking water and sprinkling powdered supplements over its fruits and vegetables. Others suggest adding vitamins only during the cold winter months.

As with humans, vitamins should not serve as an artificial replacement for a balanced diet. An overdose of vitamins can cause a great deal of damage and thus they should be administered with caution.

If your bird is a hand-fed infant, find out what the breeder gave it to eat and how long it's been weaned (never buy an unweaned infant). These babies may have additional nutritional requirements. There are various brands of prepared rearing foods available. Very young birds, as well as breeding birds and those recovering from illness may require double feedings — twice the usual amount of food.

Overleaf: 1. The cockatiel is one of the best parrots to have if breeding is your interest. But providing your tame bird with a mate will result in a loss of companionship, since the birds will pay attention to each other, not you. 2. Mutual preening is an important activity in forming the pair bond.

Feeding Schedule

Your new bird should have food provided for it round-the-clock the first day or two, but once training begins it may prove helpful to place the bird on a feeding schedule, splitting its feeding between morning and night. In the wild, cockatiels feed twice daily. It's only in captivity that they've been provided with food in such abundance.

By splitting its food supply, the cockatiel is more likely to accept food from the hand and to learn new tricks. It's suggested that the total daily supply be split into three portions: give the bird the first portion of seeds and a leafy vegetable in the morning (they seem more likely to enjoy their vegetables early in the day); the second portion should be used during training later in the day; the remaining seed and vegetables should be provided after the training is completed.

Sometimes a new bird will lose its appetite for a day or two since it is upset with having to adapt to a new environment. Ordinarily, there is nothing to worry about. If the bird is not pestered and if a food supply is readily available, the bird will eat.

You might coax it to nourishment by sprinkling some of the seed on the floor of its cage. This practice should not be continued since food on the floor can be contaminated by the bird's droppings. Sometimes, a bird will begin eating when it sees you eating.

If your bird refuses to eat after a couple of days, or if it begins to act sickly, call your veterinarian to see what he recommends.

Overleaf: This pair of cockatiels are obviously well suited for each other. However, in some cases birds put together do not get along, and a replacement must be found for one of them if breeding is to be successful. Herb Martin, a Key West breeder, recommends having three birds in a cage to ensure a suitable pair of nesting.

And if a bird you've had for some time suddenly stops eating, then you may have cause to worry since a bird's high metabolic rate can lead to a rapid and fatal weight loss. These birds, used to searching for water in their wild state, are capable of going longer without water than without seed.

Watch for other behavioral changes in a bird that's suffering from loss of appetite. Contact your vet, who may ask you to bring him in. If the bird doesn't seem to be ill, an appetite stimulant may be recommended.

Keeping Your Bird Healthy

As with all parrots, a cockatiel will provide you with tremendous amounts of joy and satisfaction, asking only a minimum of care in return. Beyond providing it with a nutritious diet and a clean, safe environment, the following tips should assure your pet has the healthiest lifestyle possible:

— Make sure your bird has several hours of total darkness. Birds, like humans, need their rest. An artificial darkness from a covered cage, though better than nothing, does not allow a bird the total rest it needs.

— There are varying thoughts on whether or not to keep a cockatiel's cage covered at night. The bird is hardy by nature and is more inclined to catch cold from a lack of vitamin A than from a draft. But if the bird seems to be stressed or slightly sick, covering the cage will help to keep it warm. It will also enable the bird to rest more easily, especially during the daytime.

Overleaf: 1. Pet cockatiels are often quite content to stay on a playground when allowed out of the cage. 2. When trimming a bird's claws, make sure you have some hydrogen peroxide handy to stop any bleeding that might occur, should you cut too much. In an emergency, flour will do the trick. 3. Medicines for simple illnesses are available at the pet store. Most are designed to be administered in the drinking water.

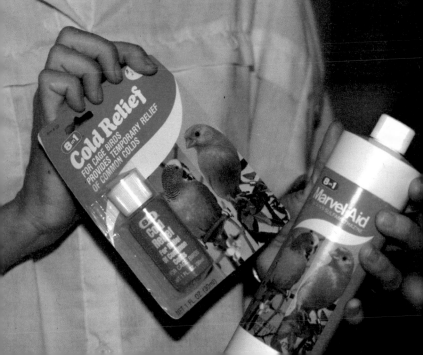

As mentioned before, each bird is unique and reacts differently to having its cage covered. For example, the first few days after bringing my cockatiel home were especially stressful for her. I found that by covering her cage, at least partially, during the day, she seemed to calm down and rest, and was even more inclined to eat and play with her new bell. And when I'm working late into the night at the desk where her cage is kept, I cover her cage with a towel to keep the light from disturbing her since she needs her rest.

— The room temperature should be kept at a comfortable level — not too hot or too cold. Sudden drops of temperature should be avoided.

— The cage should be cleaned daily. Just place a week's supply of papers on the bottom of the cage. Each day remove the top layer to rid the cage of the bird's droppings. These droppings, when dried, can blow onto the bird's food, and could cause illness. Paper towels and newspapers may be used as well as pre-cut papers found at the pet store.

Birds of Paradise pet store in Key West recommends using corn cob husks on the bottom of the cage since the soft, spongy substance is tremendously absorbent. Just by mixing it up daily, the soiled areas move to the bottom of the pile. Change the supply at least once a week.

Wash and dry the cage bottom and grill weekly with hot water and soap and sponge off cage bars periodically with plain water to keep the cage shiny and new-looking.

— Change the bird's water daily, always washing the dish thoroughly with a brush, hot water and soap. Dirty water dishes are another source of disease for the bird.

Overleaf: 1. Once a bird is hand-tame, it is easy to take it from its cage and bring it to the playground. 2. Pet cockatiels need time out of the cage for companionship as well as exercise.

The seed cup should be washed thoroughly at least twice a week, more often if the bird has soiled it. Fresh seed should be provided daily and under no circumstances allow day-old fruits, vegetables and other foods to remain in the cage.

— Keep perches clean, using sand paper, a perch scraper or a paint scraper (available from your local hardware store). If you wash the perches, dry them completely before placing them back in a cage since a wet perch leads to colds and arthritic conditions. Natural perches should be replaced every few months.

— Keep an eye out for infestations of mites and lice. If you feel your bird has external parasites, check for horizontal marks running across the heavy wing and tail feathers, an indication of lice. To check for mites, cover the cage with a white cloth at night. The tiny mites are attracted to the white cloth and will cling to it. Ordinarily, birds kept indoors will not have a parasite problem, so don't worry too much about a bird who occasionally scratches, a natural part of their preening. Keeping the cage and bird clean will prevent a parasite problem from developing.

As an extra precaution, however, there is a "bird protector" sold in pet stores that will discourage any mites or lice from establishing residence in your bird's cage.

There are commercially-prepared powders that can be used on the bird (follow directions closely so as not to harm the bird) and cage to rid them of infestations.

— When using pesticides in the house, remove the bird. Toxic fumes from insecticides, paints and the like can quickly overcome a bird.

Overleaf: 1. This cage is designed so that the door is hinged at the bottom, and a playground can be mounted on it. 2. The princess parrot is taking an interest in the pearl cockatiel.

1▲

2▼

Making Friends

If you've purchased a young bird with the intention of taming it, no doubt you're anxious to begin working with the bird as soon as you get it home.

Some bird enthusiasts recommend that you take advantage of the first hour the bird is home to make friends with it, capitalizing on the bird's disorientation and fear of the new environment. The argument is that if the bird is fearful, it may quickly come to depend on its human friends for safety.

Proponents of this school of thought also recommend beginning the taming process as soon as possible so as not to lose valuable time. Remember, the younger the bird, the easier it will be to tame it and if you buy a bird that is about six months old, valuable training time has been lost.

Others, particularly veterinarians, are more sensitive to the bird's fears, recommending that the new pet be given a day or two to get used to its new home. During this time, the bird should be placed in an area where it can get used to seeing the person designated as the primary tamer. It should not be pestered by curious family members and friends. Make no sudden or frightening moves towards the bird during this critical time for a cockatiel has a terrific memory, never forgetting someone who has scared it. This "quiet time" will enable it to get used to the normal household noises and routines.

Overleaf: Because all parrots are climbers, cages with horizontal wiring are preferable. These parrots are red-masked conures.

However, the short lives of these birds prior to being purchased are generally filled with upsetting changes — going from the nest to a cage filled with other birds and then to the life of a single, caged bird, totally isolated from its cohorts. The birds are adaptable and hardy, but a little respect for their fears goes a long way toward winning a friend.

A shy bird can be calmed by talking to it softly until it stops flying about the cage. By doing this often, the bird will soon remain on its perch when approached and may even respond with a soft chirping noise.

The "Gentle" Taming Method

There are at least two methods of taming a bird. The more gentle, time consuming approach requires a great deal of patience, but it allows the bird to become tame largely out of its own unconscious effort. The other method is quicker and simpler and is preferred by a great many bird enthusiasts.

The first method begins after a bird has become relaxed in its new environment, usually by the second day. The designated tamer should spend time talking gently to the bird, holding a hand in front of the cage in the bird's line of sight. At the first sign of panic, all movement should be stopped until the bird relaxes. After two or three days, begin moving the hand toward the bird when it preens itself, trying to lightly scratch the top of its head with your finger.

To get the bird closer to the front of the cage, try luring it with a slice of apple or millet spray or a few sprigs of seedling grass.

If the bird attempts to bite, don't pull away suddenly.

Overleaf: A group of young cockatiels: pearl pied, lutino, and pied varieties (photo by Louise Van der Meid).

You'll scare the bird and it will distrust your hand as a perch. Instinctively, a cockatiel will test the security of a perch with its beak before lighting upon it.

A very young bird's bite is relatively painless, but the older the bird, the more its bite will hurt since it holds on with rat-like tenacity. If your bird is a biter, use a twig or dull-colored pencil to scratch its head with.

Once the bird accepts having its head scratched (some birds, however, don't like to be caressed) it is all but tamed. During this phase, spend as much time as possible with the bird, moving its cage to include it in household activities.

The next stage involves getting the bird to perch on your finger. (In actual practice, this step may wind up preceding scratching the bird's head.)

First, gently open the door of the cage and slowly move your hand in with the index finger leading. Stop the movement if the cockatiel becomes excited and wait for it to relax before continuing your approach to the bird.

Keep the hand below the bird until the index finger reaches the lower part of the bird's chest. By holding the finger just above its feet, the bird finds it difficult to maintain its stance and is thus forced to step onto the finger. It may use its beak to assist itself so it is crucially important not to flinch at this point.

Once the bird is on the finger, hold the hand steady long enough for the cockatiel to relax. Then move the hand slowly toward a perch facing the bird until it is pressed lightly against the bird's chest, causing the bird to step onto the perch.

Practice this exercise several times before attempting to take the bird out of its cage. When you're ready for this step, first make sure all windows and doors are closed and no animals are in the room. This time, when the bird is perched on your hand, remove it gently from the cage. (You'll be glad you purchased a cage with a large door at this point.)

Once the bird is outside, gently scratch its head if it will allow you to, or give it a little treat of hand-held millet or grass.

Don't keep the bird out of its cage too long the first few times. But after a few short trips, return it instead to the top of its cage or to a special cockatiel playground available from your pet store.

Once taming has progressed this far, you may want to teach it to accept being carried without a struggle. When putting the bird back into its cage, perched upon your finger, just use your other hand to lightly envelop the bird. Hold it closely enough to keep it from flying off, but loosely enough to keep from frightening it.

During the taming process, it is likely the bird will be startled and will fly away, hence the need to ensure all windows and doors are closed. To prevent possible injury, cover windows and mirrors until the bird learns the geography of the room. Don't chase a bird while it is in flight, or you may cause it to injure itself by flying into a wall or other object.

Instead, wait for it to land and then approach it cautiously, but with little delay to get it to perch on your finger.

Once tamed by this gentle method, the bird can be allowed out of its cage at any time, but never go outside with a bird on your shoulder unless you're prepared for the risk of having it fly away.

An Alternative Method

The second taming method, which is supposed to

Overleaf: 1. The ability to fly depends mostly on the outer feathers of the wing. Trimming these feathers will keep the bird from flying. 2. A cockatiel cage must at the very least be furnished with cups for seed and water.

1▲   2▼

have a bird perched on your finger in an hour or less, relies largely on making the bird flightless by clipping one or both of its wings. With this procedure, allowing the bird full use of its wings guarantees wasted time chasing the bird, and causes unnecessary stress from the fright of being pursued.

This taming procedure begins by placing the bird in a small room such as a bathroom or hallway, one that is isolated from the rest of the house. Again, all windows and mirrors should be covered and any dangerous items removed since the bird is likely to be all over the taming area. Hard floor coverings should be cushioned to protect the bird from injury.

The cockatiel, unable to fly because of its clipped wing, is gently taken in the hand. Though a glove may be used to protect the hand from what might be a painful bite, it is not recommended as it will frighten the bird, and, it is more difficult to gauge the pressure exerted on the bird when it is being held.

Bringing the bird low to the ground, slowly relax your hold, allowing the bird to flutter to the ground. As it lands, encircle the bird with ungloved hands lying flat on the floor, making it necessary for the bird to step on your fingers if it wants to escape. If it jumps off your fingers, encircle the bird again, repeating this corraling process slowly and gently until the bird feels secure on its human perch.

Again, don't jerk away if the bird attempts to bite you. In most cases, the bite won't hurt and only serves

Overleaf: 1. A nest box attached to the side of the cage or aviary should be about 12 x 12 x 10 inches, with a 3-inch entrance hole. Wood chips on the floor of the box will provide a cushion for the eggs. 2. The markings of the pied variety, shown on the left, can often be striking.

in letting the bird know that your hand is a secure perch.

Once the bird is relaxed on your finger, slowly bring the index finger of the other hand gently into contact with the bird's chest. The bird, feeling off-balance, will step onto that finger. Repeating this process again and again, creating a "ladder" effect of getting the bird to step from hand to hand, is a good taming exercise. It is best to conduct this exercise just above floor level, continuing to talk softly to the bird. After a while, the exercise can be continued with others participating, ensuring the bird will not be a one-person pet.

If the bird is young, two hours is all it needs to be tamed by this process, claim the advocates of this method.

In the two weeks following the initial taming session, the designated tamer should spend some time each day with the bird on his hand, perhaps scratching its head. After a few days, the tameness should be irreversible as long as human contact is continued.

Before long, the bird should be anxious to spend time with you, climbing from your shoulder to the top of your head, asking for affection and, in return, keeping you entertained with its amusing antics.

If, however, after trying either of these methods you are unable to tame your bird, you may want to consider getting another one. But if you have not adhered to a training schedule, there is no point in getting a new bird.

A reputable pet shop will sometimes let you trade in an untamable bird on another one or at least will give you partial credit toward the purchase of a new one.

Overleaf: 1. Once a bird is tame enough to sit on your finger, it is ready to accept affection and may be willing to learn to mimic words. 2, 3. Training tapes and records are available from the pet store. They can lessen the tedious chore of repeating words or phrases you want the bird to learn.

Catching an Escaped Bird

Catching an untamed bird with a clipped wing is best done with a net placed gently over it. A towel may also be used to gently wrap around the bird. If the bird gets outside, catch it as quickly as possible to prevent it from being injured by predators or from getting so far away you'll never catch it.

If it lands in a tree out of range, place its cage with food, water and millet spray in full view. If you have another cockatiel, place it (in its own cage) next to the empty cage to lure the escaped bird and then just wait.

A Third Way — Your Own Method

As pointed out previously, every bird is unique and responds differently to attempts to tame it. After talking with pet store owners and breeders and doing my reading, I decided to try the second method of taming Pearl. I let the pet store clip her wings rather than attempt it myself and, sure enough, within five minutes she was sitting on my finger.

But when I got her home, she was most unwilling to repeat the exercise. So I decided, upon the advice of the pet store, to use a more gentle means of continuing the taming process.

I had already noticed that she seemed spunkier, more adventuresome early in the morning, which is the bird's normal singing time. So I used that time of day to work with her.

Instead of placing my hand in her cage, forcing her to come out and scaring her in the process, I left her cage door open and just talked gently to her. I kept up my end of the converstaion even when I was away from the cage, getting ready for work. She always sat on the

Overleaf: The subtle colors found in lutino cockatiels (1) are at the opposite extreme from more brilliantly colored parrots (2).

perch closest to the front of the cage where she could keep a close eye on me.

I then borrowed a portion of the first taming method noted above and began moving my index finger slowly toward her at perch level. As soon as she began to panic, racing to the back of the cage, I stopped all movement. Within seconds she was back at the front of the cage watching me. This exercise required patience and some time, but within a few days, instead of running to the back of the cage, she would hop onto the cage door (which opens outwardly, providing a flat perch).

From there, she began to let me place my hands around her feet (as recommended in the second method) so that she could walk onto my hand. Though the first few days I learned the hard way that some older cockatiels do have a vicious bite, I learned not to flinch when she made a move toward my finger. Within a week, as she grew to trust my finger perch, her biting stopped.

At first she didn't like to ride on my shoulder, but after repeatedly placing her there, she has grown to enjoy riding around the house with me as I do my daily chores.

I also found that if she seemed excited and about ready to fly off my shoulder or finger, I would stand in front of a mirror and talk gently to her. She seemed to enjoy the image of another bird with me and it calmed her down for a while.

The first few times I had her out of the cage for short periods of time (less than 30 minutes), but as she became calmer the time was extended to an hour. Again, by watching her to see if she was overly agitated or excited, I could determine how long to keep her out. And if the next day she seemed particularly upset with the idea of going

Overleaf: Clipping the feathers of at least one wing is often necessary before a cockatiel can be tamed. The wing trim shown here, and favored by Birds of Paradise, involves cutting several of the outermost feathers of the wing.

1▲ 2▼

through the taming exercise, I postponed the session. The following day she was always ready for a new adventure.

The method I wound up using is really a combination of the recommended taming methods and my own common sense after having watched my bird's habits. The critical keys are patience and respect for the cockatiel you hope to have for a longtime companion.

Clipping the Wings

Clipping a bird's wing to make it easier to tame only temporarily interferes with their flight capabilities. In fact, the cockatiel is such a terrific flyer, it can learn to cope with one clipped wing though its flight will be off-balance. A bird with two clipped wings can quickly learn to fly, but some advocates of the two-wing clip believe it is kinder to the bird than to have it condemned to a few months of lop-sided flight. Clipping wings is unnecessary for hand-fed cockatiels. Once the bird is tamed, you can decide whether to keep the wing clipped, repeating the process about every six months.

A pet shop will help you with clipping before taking the bird home, although the procedure is simple enough for you to do yourself. But since a bird may associate you with the unpleasant experience of being constrained during clipping, it is recommended that someone else do it.

To clip a bird's flight feathers, get a good, light pair of clippers (small wire cutters), scissors and some "Kwik Stop" or hydrogen peroxide in case of bleeding.

Make sure you can recognize blood feathers from those feathers that can be clipped. Blood feathers have not finished growing and thus have a blood vessel in the shaft to provide nourishment directly from the bird's

Overleaf: 1. Trimming the feathers just beyond the feathers that overlap above is usually sufficient. 2. This wing trim is not unattractive, since the feather sections lost are hidden when the wings are folded.

vascular system. If a blood feather is accidentally clipped, stop the bleeding immediately since a cockatiel can bleed to death in minutes.

It is easier and safer for the bird if two people participate in the clipping process. The person holding the bird should watch the bird's respiration and keep the bird still, using two hands to hold the bird. The bird's body should be supported on your lap or on a towel-covered counter. The bird's head and neck should be kept straight and it should not be allowed to twist its body. Just place a thumb under the lower mandible with the rest of the fingers around the head, using the other hand to hold the bird's feet and torso.

Let the more experienced person clip the wing. Begin by extending the wing to give full view of the feathers. Push back the under-coverts to fully expose the feather shafts, checking for blood feathers before proceeding. Then first use the scissors to cut in half only the third and fourth feathers, leaving the first two feathers intact. Take the clippers and clip the next 8 to 10 feathers just where the feather emerges from the shaft, leaving ¾-inch of feather shaft.

Training the Bird to Talk

Once a cockatiel is tame enough to comfortably sit on your finger and to accept the affection you have to offer it, you may want to take advantage of this parrot's ability to learn to mimic words and whistles. This is only possible with single birds isolated from others.

A cockatiel's "voice" is not as humanlike or distinctive as that of the African Grey Parrot. It has a reedy sort of sound, much like a child's voice and more similar to that of the budgerigars.

And not all cockatiels are trainable, with some "smarter" than others. Only patience and time will tell.

Cockatiels have an easier time learning words with

Above: The white wing patch found in the wild-colored cockatiel persists in the pearl variety (photo by Dr. Herbert R. Axelrod). Facing page: A cockatiel—in this case, a pearl—can obtain necessary calcium from a Nylabird toy, a cuttlebone, or a mineral block.

many vowels such as "hello" or "coco" and once it learns a single word, it is easier to pick up other sounds. But it must frequently review anything it has learned or it will forget its previous vocabulary.

Begin teaching your bird its first word by speaking slowly and distinctly, working on only one new word at a time. Choose training times early in the morning and late in the afternoon — the natural song times for a bird.

As it is more natural for the cockatiel to mimic whistles, it is often easier to train it to repeat melodious sounds.

All training requires a patient person willing to work with the bird on a frequent basis for short intervals of time. The desired word or phrases must be repeated numerous times, preferably by a woman or child since their voice more closely resembles a cockatiel's.

Some people leave the training to tapes or records that are available at pet stores since the monotonous repetition required is enough to discourage even the most enthusiastic trainer. Others record their own voice.

Teaching a bird to do tricks such as climbing ropes and ladders or retrieving seeds and objects from a container requires a system of rewards where undesirable behavior is ignored and desired behavior wins food and praise to reinforce repetition.

How long it takes to train a cockatiel depends on the bird's capacity for learning and on your willingness to devote the time necessary on a regular basis.

As with taming your bird, don't overdo the lessons. Daily sessions for short periods of three to five minutes get better results than hours spent listening to your voice. A frustrated trainer who insists on overdoing the lessons will only prove stressful to your bird, who may have other ideas on how to spend his day.

Caring for the Sick or Injured Bird

An ounce of prevention goes a long way toward keeping your bird healthy and alive for the full lifespan of about 20 years.

As one vet said, it is unfortunately true that a bird is taken to the doctor only when it is sick. Instead, it should be checked annually by a qualified vet to assure the bird is healthy and that you are caring for it appropriately.

As with humans, even the best-cared-for bird may acquire a disease or injury so it's important to learn some of the symptoms of a sick bird.

The clever cockatiel instinctively will hide its sickness from you for as long as possible. This is because in the wild, the sick, weak animals are those that fall victim to predators. So the parrot "fakes" normalcy for as long as possible.

Though this may save its life in the wild, it may lead to its death in captivity since a bird who is too sick to carry on this charade is often too sick to be helped, even by the best of veterinarians.

The better you learn your bird's habits, recognizing a change in pattern, the faster you'll be able to get medical attention if needed.

Common Warning Signs
Here are some common warning signs:

Above: A wild-colored female cockatiel (photo by Dr. Herbert R. Axelrod). Facing page: With wild-colored adults, the bright colors of the male's head most easily distinguishes him from a female (photo by Nancy Richmond).

1) A change in the bird's attitude such as apathy and lethargy.

2) A change in the volume, texture and color of the bird's droppings (in a day's time, one bird should have about 20 droppings which should be dark green and white in color and of a fairly thick consistency, not runny).

3) A change in food and water consumption.

4) A change in the bird's appearance — ruffled feathers, runny eyes or nostrils, difficulty in maintaining its usual erect posture.

5) A change in the bird's activities — talking and whistling less than normal, little response to stimuli.

6) Difficulty in breathing with respiratory sounds such as sneezing, wheezing or clicking.

7) Any noticeable enlargement on the bird's body — fat is abnormal on a bird.

If your bird exhibits any of these symptoms, it may be time to call a veterinarian for some advice.

The doctor may recommend using some of the antibiotics available at the pet store or other remedies for colds and digestive disorders.

Hospital Cages

Because a sick bird is easily chilled, it will often respond to treatment in a heated "hospital cage."

Specially-made hospital cages are available at pet stores, or you can turn your bird's cage into a care shelter by simply placing a heating pad on the floor of the cage, covered of course.

Turn the heating pad on to medium heat and cover most of the cage to keep the warmth in, allowing an area for fresh air to get through so that the bird has some choice as to where to sit to be the most comfortable. The temperature inside the cage should remain at about 85 degrees.

Some aviculturists recommend making a hospital

cage using a low-watt bulb and a rheostat so that the level of lighting can be adjusted to keep the temperature at the desired level. But others fear the brightness of the light prevents the bird from getting its needed rest.

In fact, a sick bird, like a human, may need up to 16 hours of rest a day with a mid-day nap thrown in for good measure. So keeping the bird in a darkened room to ensure quiet is advised.

When to See a Vet

If your bird fails to respond fairly quickly to these treatments, then take him to the vet. A sick bird may fail rapidly and there is little time to waste in seeking treatment for your bird.

An injury that causes bleeding should be quickly cared for as a cockatiel has very little blood in its vascular system and can quickly bleed to death. Pack the bleeding area with "Kwik Stop" or hydrogen peroxide. If first aid medication is not readily available, use flour to help stop the bleeding.

In some cases, stitches may be required or a broken bone may have to be set — both procedures should be done only by a vet. If an injury results in the amputation of an appendage, the bird will likely adjust to its new limitations as long as you protect it from predators that might take advantage of its handicap.

Diseases

The most dreaded disease feared by all bird lovers is psittacosis (parrot disease as it's sometimes called). More correctly it is called ornithosis (bird disease) since it is not limited to the parrot family.

This disease can be transmitted to man, manifesting itself as a flu-like illness that has been known to cause death. However, medical advances in antibiotics for both bird and man have made it a curable disease and it

Above: Tame cockatiels, like this female, are easier to care for because they can be handled readily (photo by E. J. Mulawka). Facing page: Careful attention to your bird's appearance is the best way to detect illness early (photo by Vincent Serbin).

is no longer necessary to destroy entire collections of birds as in the past.

This disease is difficult to diagnose in birds since symptoms such as excessive sleepiness, diarrhea or pneumonia among birds is observed only in cases of very severe infection. But any bird breeder who has a high rate of mortality among his birds should have the dead birds examined. If psittacosis is diagnosed, the authorities must be notified to prevent the disease from spreading to other bird colonies.

A good reference to have on hand is *Bird Diseases* by Heinz-Sigurd Raethel, which provides an explanation of a wide range of ailments and their treatments.

Other Health Problems

Health problems caused by a dirty environment can be easily prevented by regular cleaning of the cage bottom and aviary floor, with disinfecting recommended at least twice a year.

Without cleaning, mites, bacteria and worms proliferate, potentially harming your pet.

Mites and lice infestations can be treated with a commercial spray or powder (non-oil-based) but great care should be taken to protect the eyes, head and beak from the toxic substance. The whole cage or aviary must be treated at the same time.

Bird breeders may have a problem with worms that are transmitted through the excreta of free-living birds or infested new arrivals. Birds infested with worms soon grow weak, losing their resistance to what might have been a simple cold and other illnesses.

As a preventive measure, birds may be wormed twice a year, using an anthelminthic mixed into the drinking water of the bird. With this treatment, the cockatiel's drinking water is withheld two days prior to the treatment along with all other foods with a high water content to encourage the bird to drink the required amount of treated water.

Though not a disease, molting -- the normal change of plumage twice a year — can place a strain on the bird's resistance to disease. Thus it is especially important during this time that the bird's diet be rich in vitamins. If an intermediate molt occurs due to frequent changes in room temperatures or drafts, there should be nothing to worry about.

Clipping the Nails

A pet cockatiel allowed to roam about the house and furnishings may do some damage if it nails are allowed to grow. The bird may injure itself if its claws get stuck just as it's about to take flight.

By providing the bird with natural wood perches, this should not be a problem. If, however, the claws become overgrown to the point of curling, they should be clipped cautiously with great care taken to avoid cutting the vein.

The nail clipping procedure should be done in a good light so that the vessels in the nails can be easily seen. One person should hold the bird firmly but gently, isolating a foot so the clippers can be used to just barely snip the tip of each claw.

In case a blood vessel is nicked, have some "Kwik Stop," hydrogen peroxide or an antiseptic first aid powder on hand to quickly stop the bleeding.

A preferable method of keeping the claws in shape is to file the rough edges, a procedure often allowed by a very tame bird.

Beak Trimming

An overgrown beak — a rarity in birds provided with cuttlebone, Nylabird and other chewing materials — must also be trimmed or filed to keep it from interfering with normal eating. To file the mandible (beak), the

Above: A pied cockatiel enjoys the ladder part of its playground (photo by Nancy Richmond). Facing page: Young cockatiels, pied and lutino (photo by Louise Van der Meid).

bird's head should be held between the thumb and index finger, thus preventing the bird from biting.

The bird may be kept from biting during the procedure by inserting a small twig between the upper and lower mandibles and allowing the bird to bite down. Before filing, rub the mandible with cooking oil to keep it from splintering or tearing.

Dealing with a Dead Bird

Sometimes, no matter how well you care for your bird, your cockatiel will succumb to age, disease or injury.

If you have other birds and you fear a contagious disease caused the death, it would be wise to take the dead bird to a veterinarian so that an examination can be made to determine cause of death. If some of the bird's droppings are available, take them with you since the excrement may provide valuable information on what caused your bird to die.

In homes where children have come to love the bird, its death can cause a great upset. As with other types of pets, the loss of your bird may prompt your youngster to ask questions about death. (This is a good opportunity to explain simply your own views of death, taking care to provide simple answers that address what the child has asked — no more or less.)

How you handle your bird's death will help pattern your child's means of dealing with the inevitable loss of loved ones throughout his or her life.

If the youngster would like to bury the bird, simply find a sturdy box to place it in. Let the child decide where the bird should be buried and then proceed with the service, allowing the child to determine as much as possible how the funeral should be conducted.

Some people who are particularly attached to their pet parrot have been known to contact a local taxidermist to have it stuffed, thus forever preserving its beauty.

Breeding Your Cockatiel

The cockatiel is perhaps one of the best birds to have if breeding is what you're interested in. These birds have acquired a reputation over the past century of being fairly easy to breed in captivity, producing several young each year in the proper environment.

But take heed — if you choose to breed your tame cockatiel, you risk losing the companionship of your bird since once they begin raising a family, the instinctive need to protect the nest takes over. You're better off buying other birds for breeding purposes, perhaps selecting the more common gray cockatiels for your first efforts since they are more easily sexed.

By selecting healthy, unrelated mature birds over a year old, you will avoid such side effects as unfertilized clutches, incomplete incubations and improper care of the young. Not all male and female matches are "made in heaven." As with humans, some cockatiels are very selective in choosing a suitable mate. Some breeders recommend that three birds be placed in a cage, improving the odds that at least two of them are suitable mates.

If your pair doesn't seem to be hitting it off, try exchanging one of them for another of the same sex. Remove particularly aggressive males.

Nesting Box

Provide the breeding pair with a separate nesting box to the side of the cage or aviary. Nesting boxes made of wood and sized specifically for cockatiels (12'' x 12'' x

Above: A wild cockatiel at a cavity in a tree limb (photo by Ken Stepnell). Facing page: In lutino cockatiels the amount of yellow in the plumage varies considerably from bird to bird, though in all of them the head and crest are the yellowest parts of the body (photo by Glen Axelrod).

10" with a three-inch entrance hole) are available at most pet stores or from local breeders. Wood chips should be used on the floor of the nesting box to provide adequate cushion for the eggs and to help retain the moisture necessary to prevent the eggs from drying out.

If you'd like to build your own nest box, choose materials that don't smell brand new, using chipboard or wood.

Diet

Make sure your breeding cockatiels have been receiving a proper diet for at least six months prior to mating since nesting, egg laying and rearing the young stress both parents' systems. A proper diet will also help prevent the hen from being egg bound, and the parents will be better prepared to feed their young.

Breeding Season

In the wild, cockatiels breed year-around, depending on climatic conditions and the availability of food and water. In captivity, a typical breeding season is between August and December with some birds successfully mating as early as April. Often breeders will foster breeding in October in order to have plenty of babies available for Christmas gifts. In warmer climates such as Florida or Hawaii where breeding occurs year-around, the pairs are often separated during the hot summer months when temperatures in the nesting boxes can get extremely high.

Once the nest boxes are hung, the pair will soon embark on their courtship with the cock displaying his yellow crest and slightly spread wings, walking about the hen with quick, small steps. He may try to attract her attention by lowering his head and spreading his tail feathers out like a fan, emitting a loud whistle at the same time.

If the hen is willing, copulation follows and if all goes well, she will begin laying her eggs about 10 to 15 days later. She will lay a single egg every other day until the clutch is complete with four to seven eggs. Incubation requires 20 to 23 days with both birds brooding — the male during the daylight hours and the female at night. You'll know when the eggs hatch from the funny, croaking sounds the young will make. When hatched, they'll be covered in a pale yellow down with a bald patch at the back of their heads.

Once the eggs hatch, keep an eye out to assure the parents are caring properly for the babies. If not, hand-feeding may be required to keep the babies alive though this should be avoided since parent-raised infants are hardier.

Caring for Neglected Offspring

Neglected offspring that have to be hand-fed should be placed in an incubator with a temperature stablized at 95 degrees.

(You can create your own incubator by placing a small, napkin-lined cardboard box containing the chicks into the bottom of a slightly larger box. On the bottom of the larger box, place a hot water bottle or a heating pad (on medium heat). Drape both boxes with a towel to retain the heat. Keep the temperature about 95 to 100 degrees Fahrenheit for chicks in their first week. Drop the temperature to 80 degrees the next two weeks. After that, if the chicks appear to be too hot, panting or turning pink in color, drop the temperature by 5 degrees.)

The baby bird should be handled as little as possible and should be removed from the warmth of the incubator only during feeding (every two to three hours for the first four days; every four hours for the five-to-nine-day-old bird; and every six hours for the remainder of the hand-feeding). Never skip a meal for these dependent chicks and if your schedule is too busy to be com-

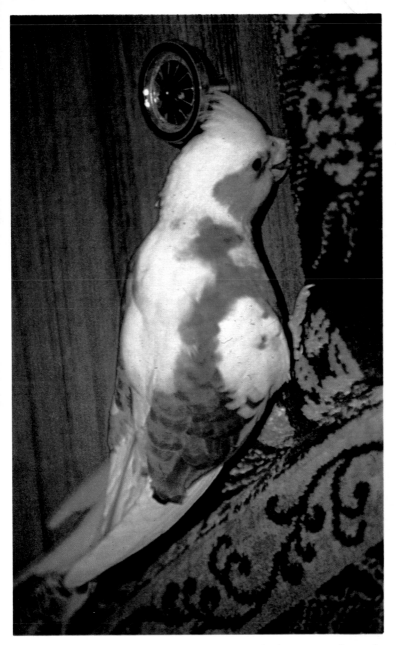

Above: Cockatiels are inclined to chew; this pied youngster is ready to take on the sofa (photo by Ray Hanson). Facing page: Young cockatiels in a pet shop—note the corn cob on the floor (photo by Louise Van der Meid).

mitted to the demanding feeding schedule, arrange for someone else to assure the chicks are fed.

The hand-fed baby should be given a special diet available at most pet stores. Or else you can make your own food by toasting whole wheat bread and crumbling it in a dish. Add sunflower or millet meal, cod liver oil, prepared baby peas or green beans, baby food, grated carrots and a few drops of vitamins along with some warm water to create a soft and crumbly mix.

Using a small plastic syringe or spoon, fill the baby's crop up, trying to keep out excess air without squeezing the chick.

Baby Birds Grow Rapidly

When fed properly, both hand-fed and parent-fed babies grow rapidly and may begin investigating the world outside of their nest at four weeks of age. Pin feathers develop after seven days with wing, tail and crest feathers appearing first. Their eyes open at the age of five to 10 days, and this is the period recommended for placing a permanent identification band about their leg. After about 18 days, the spots of their cheeks begin to develop and by four weeks, the plumage is fully developed.

The babies usually leave their nest after five to six weeks. Weaning begins at this point with most babies eating on their own by eight weeks of age.

Before separating the babies from their parents, make sure they are eating independently or they may become ill. At 10 weeks, the infants are usually ready for taming as family pets but are still a bit young to be transported to a pet store for sale.

In General

A good breeding pair will produce two to three broods a year, often resulting in as many as 15 young birds. After each brood, the nest box should be cleaned thoroughly to prevent pests from infesting the nest area.

After the third and final brood (no more than three broods a year is advisable) the nest box should be removed and disinfected.

The young from the previous hatch should be removed from the cage before the next brood hatches since they may disturb the rearing of the new chicks.

Breeding birds isn't for everyone but for those who choose to try it, it can be a very rewarding experience. However, if all does not go well and hand-feeding is required, the schedule demanded for caring for the offspring can be grueling. You may have to call on friends and family members to help out. But the reward comes in having a loving bird that is extremely tame, having learned to trust the hand that fed it.

Breeding for Color Variations

More advanced breeders may attempt to pair their birds so as to acquire a number of color mutations that have evolved over the past several years. Thanks to a century of concerted breeding efforts and the increasing knowledge available regarding genetics, the cockatiel now comes in a variety of colors, including white, yellow, pied, pearled, bordered, cream and cinnamon as well as the traditional gray.

Though various mutations have occurred sporadically, careful selective breeding has "fixed" or stabilized only these few color varieties. In the wild, color mutations quickly disappeared since the birds were more easily spotted by their natural predators than the gray birds who blended into the landscape.

Before embarking on a search for a new color mutation, or on breeding one of the more rare color forms, it would be helpful to do some research into genetics. Detailed records of breeding efforts should be kept in order to select suitable birds from among the descen-

Above: Cockatiel chick, three weeks old (photo by Bruce D. Lavoy).
Facing page: Gray, or wild-colored, cockatiels, both males (photo
by Nancy Richmond).

dants for further breeding.

Some of the variations possible in breeding are the following:

— Gray or "wild" colored cockatiels are the most common birds available. They are needed in the breeding of mutations to improve the type and size of the cockatiels.

— White cockatiels with red eyes (albinos), which first made their debut in 1959, are regarded by some as the first mutation. In its early stages, the variation fetched fantastic prices but ease of breeding this type bird has forced the price down so that now the cost is little more than a gray. These white birds have the lemon-yellow head and peach cheek patches as well as delicate yellow feathers on the underside of the tail.

— White cockatiels with black eyes were bred soon after their red-eyed counterparts. In addition to having black eyes, these albino birds seem to have whiter, brighter plumage.

— Yellow cockatiels are often referred to as lutinos, a word derived from Latin which means "yellow lipochrome." It is the lipochrome pigment which gives the lutinos their yellow color.

— Pearled cockatiels were first bred in Europe. These birds have a light gray plumage dappled with white to yellowish spots of color on the upper side and wings. The crest is grayish yellow with yellow rump, tail feathers and under-tail coverts. Unfortunately, the intensive coloration of these unusual birds diminishes with age, most notably in the male, which may revert to a gray coloration by the age of one year.

— Bordered cockatiels are similar to the pearled except the pearled feathers in the plumage of back and wings have a dark or light margin. Again, this color mutation has the disadvantage of fading colors with increasing age.

— The pied cockatiels were first bred about the same time as the albinos and today are possible in a variety of colors. The pied or harlequin spots should be symmetrical and distinct though pied markings range from lightly flecked plumage to those that are nearly all white with a few gray feathers.

— The cinnamon (isabel) cockatiels are also referred to as silvers. Their forehead and head feathers are lemon-colored with the shafts of the crest a brownish shade, becoming yellowish as they approach the tip. The ear patches are reddish orange with the rest of the plumage a brownish color — thus the cinnamon appearance.

Exhibiting Your Bird

Aviculturists interested in showing their favorite cockatiel may enter the bird in official American Cockatiel Society exhibitions. Each year, an increasing number of breeding clubs and local branches of the society arrange for such exhibitions of a variety of birds, particularly the parakeet, African lovebirds and cockatiels.

One must become a member of the ACS in order to enter the exhibits where birds are judged on the basis of a point system. Membership in this organization authorizes breeders to use authorized breeder bands that bear the membership number of the breeder, the year the birds were bred and an identification serial number.

These exhibitions enable a breeder to compare birds raised by other aviculturists, a necessary practice in striving for the ideal bird prescribed by the ACS standards. Trained judges can objectively evaluate a cockatiel, suggesting ways of improving the stock so as to produce an even hardier, more beautiful bird.

Such shows are also a good source of the most up-to-date information available on the caring and breeding of cockatiels.

Above: Tame cockatiels will readily climb a chain (photo by Nancy Richmond). Facing page: On this male, the outermost feathers of both wings have been trimmed (photo by Nancy Richmond).

Conclusion

I hope the information provided is helpful to you. Using the advice of those experienced in raising cockatiels to help me with my own cockatiel has given me a whole new perspective on how truly enjoyable these parrots can be.

As Joe Pigeon and John Smithers of *Birds of Paradise* pet store recommended, I've come to respect my bird. I've learned her routine. And by paying attention to such details as when she likes to eat or when she takes an afternoon nap, I can schedule my time of working with her.

Rather than intrude on her "safe" space — the cage — by forcing her to come out, I've used gentle coaxing. Slowly, she has started to come out of her cage on her own. Though she hasn't yet mastered climbing onto my finger without a fuss, she's less inclined to bite me and appears to be much more relaxed once she is on my hand or shoulder.

I don't think it was an accident that I got a cockatiel who was feisty and not easily tamed. Though most young birds (under six months old) will be easily finger-tamed, my Pearl is a biter. Taming her has required patience and, as I said, respect for her own routine.

But she does seem to be fascinated with whatever is going on in the room, sitting on the perch at the front of her cage where she can get the best view.

And whenever I've had a question, the pet store where I bought the cockatiel has been more than willing to help me out. That's one of the advantages of going to a good pet store where the personnel are qualified and care enough to help out a new bird owner.

I hope you'll find as I have that cockatiels are a perfect pet — they're hardy, affectionate, attractive and smart. They're easy to take care of and generally they'll provide companionship for many years — provided you take the minimal amount of time and effort necessary to care for them properly.